A MESSAGE TO PARENTS

Reading good books to young children is a crucial factor in a child's psychological and intellectual development. It promotes a mutually warm and satisfying relationship between parent and child and enhances the child's awareness of the world around him. It stimulates the child's imagination and lays a foundation for the development of the skills necessary to support the critical thinking process. In addition, the parent who reads to his child helps him to build vocabulary and other prerequisite skills for the child's own successful reading.

In order to provide parents and children with books which will do these things, Brown Watson has published this series of small books specially designed for young children. These books are factual, fanciful, humorous, questioning and adventurous. A library acquired in this inexpensive way will provide many hours of pleasurable and profitable reading for parents and children.

Published by Brown Watson (Leicester) Ltd.
ENGLAND
© 1980 Rand McNally & Company
Printed and bound in the German Democratic Republic.

HUMPTY DUMPTY
and other Mother Goose Rhymes

Illustrated by

MARY JANE CHASE

Brown Watson

England.

HUMPTY DUMPTY

Humpty Dumpty sat on a wall;
Humpty Dumpty had a great fall.
All the king's horses
　　　and all the king's men
Couldn't put Humpty together
　　　again.

THE LITTLE GIRL WITH A CURL

There was a little girl
     who had a little curl
Right in the middle
     of her forehead;
When she was good,
     she was very, very good,
And when she was bad,
     she was horrid.

HANDY PANDY

Handy Pandy, Jack-a-dandy,
Loves plum cake and sugar candy.
He bought some at a grocer's shop,
And out he came, hop, hop, hop!

BOW-WOW-WOW

Bow-wow-wow!
Whose dog art thou?
Little Tom Tinker's dog,
Bow-wow-wow!

POLLY AND SUKEY

Polly, put the kettle on,
Polly, put the kettle on,
Polly, put the kettle on,
We'll all have tea.

Sukey, take it off again,
Sukey, take it off again,
Sukey, take it off again,
They've all gone away.

GEORGY PORGY

Georgy Porgy, pudding and pie,
Kissed the girls and made them cry.
When the boys came out to play,
Georgy Porgy ran away.

THREE WISE MEN OF GOTHAM

Three wise men of Gotham
Went to sea in a bowl;
If the bowl had been stronger,
My song had been longer.

OH, DEAR

Dear, dear! what can the matter be ?
Two old women got up in an
      apple tree;
One came down, and the other
      stayed till Saturday.

LITTLE JACK HORNER

Little Jack Horner sat in the corner,
Eating a Christmas pie:
   He put in his thumb,
    And pulled out a plum,
And said, "What a good boy am I!"

MY KITTEN

Hey, my kitten, my kitten,
　And hey, my kitten, my deary!
Such a sweet pet as this
　Was neither far nor neary.

ONE MISTY MOISTY MORNING

One misty moisty morning,
   When cloudy was the weather,
I chanced to meet an old man,
   Clothed all in leather.
He began to compliment
   And I began to grin.
How do you do And how do you do?
   And how do you do again?

THE CAT AND THE FIDDLE

Hey, diddle, diddle!
The cat and the fiddle,
The cow jumped over the moon;
The little dog laughed
To see such sport,
And the dish ran away with the
spoon.

THE MAN OF BOMBAY

There was a fat man of Bombay,
Who was smoking one sunshiny
day;
When a bird called a snipe
Flew away with his pipe,
Which vexed the fat man of
Bombay.

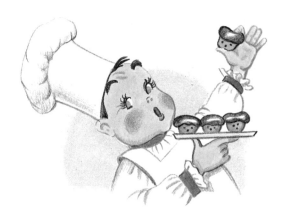

Hot-cross buns!
Hot-cross buns!
One a penny, two a penny,
Hot-cross buns!

If you have no daughters,
Give them to your sons.
One a penny, two a penny,
Hot-cross buns!

PETER PIPER

Peter Piper picked a peck of pickled
      peppers;
A peck of pickled peppers Peter
      Piper picked.
If Peter Piper picked a peck of
      pickled peppers,
Where's the peck of pickled
      peppers Peter Piper picked?

JACK AND JILL

Jack and Jill went up the hill
    To fetch a pail of water;
Jack fell down and broke his crown,
    And Jill came tumbling after.

SING A SONG OF SIXPENCE

Sing a song of sixpence,
A pocket full of rye;
Four-and-twenty blackbirds
Baked in a pie!

When the pie was opened,
The birds began to sing;
Was not that a dainty dish
To set before the king?

The king was in his
    counting-house,
  Counting out his money;
The queen was in the parlour,
  Eating bread and honey;

The maid was in the garden,
  Hanging out the clothes;
When down came a blackbird
  And snapped off her nose.

BARBER, BARBER

Barber, barber, shave a pig.
How many hairs will make a wig?
Four and twenty; that's enough.
Give the barber a pinch of snuff.

THE MAN IN THE MOON

The Man in the Moon came
tumbling down,
And asked the way to Norwich;
He went by the south, and burnt
his mouth
With eating cold pease porridge.

A SURE TEST

If you are to be a gentleman,
  As I suppose you'll be,
You'll neither laugh nor smile,
  For a tickling of the knee.

PUSSY-CAT, PUSSY-CAT

"Pussy-cat, pussy-cat,
  Where have you been?"
"I've been to London
  To look at the Queen."

"Pussy-cat, pussy-cat,
  What did you there?"
"I frightened a little mouse
  Under her chair."

FIVE TOES

This little pig went to market;
This little pig stayed at home;
This little pig had roast beef;
This little pig had none;
This little pig cried, "Wee, wee!"
All the way home.